RICHARD PEARSON'S
WELTON SKETCHB

C000184674

for Jen, with love

*A Limited edition of 1500 copies of which the first 500 are numbered
and signed by the Author*

Hutton Press
1996

ACKNOWLEDGEMENTS

Many people have contributed to the making of this Welton Sketchbook. I should like to thank all of them and in particular Neville and Betty Snowden, Anne Bousfield and Trevor Hulse for supplying much useful information as well as patiently answering my questions.

My thanks also to the East Yorkshire Local History Society for permission to quote from Dr. Allison's book, "Hull Gent Seeks Country Residence". Certain information has also been taken from Thomas Thompson's book, "Welton and its Neighbourhood" published in 1869. Much else has been gleaned from Weltonians and my sincere thanks to them all.

Published by
The Hutton Press Ltd.,
130 Canada Drive, Cherry
Burton, Beverley, East
Yorkshire
HU17 7SB

Copyright 1996

Printed by
Burstwick Print & Publicity
Services,
13a Anlaby Road, Hull
HU1 2PJ

ISBN   1 872167 89 6

No part of this book may be reproduced, stored in a retrieval system or transmitted in any form, or by any means electronic, mechanical photocopying, recording or otherwise without the prior permission of the Publisher and the Copyright holder.

FOREWORD

This is not a history of Welton but as I made the drawings in this book I wished to discover something of their story in the life of the village. Having lived 'only' sixteen years in Welton I have still much to learn about the place so naturally I asked Weltonians what they know. Unlike the 'southerner' who attended a Roses cricket match and on inquiring as to the state of the game had the reply, "It's nowt to do wi'thee!", I have had much help and encouragement from the natives.

Thanks to Conservation Area status and the official Listing of numerous buildings Welton has not been the victim of wholesale modern development. Unlike many local villages that have been subjected to unsympathetic treatment Welton has managed to change with the times whilst retaining its character along with its attractive properties many of which have been restored and preserved by conscientious owners.

In making this sketchbook I selected the subjects initially for their picturesque appeal. As the number of drawings increased I realised that though some were less picturesque than others, all were important in Welton's story, so like Topsy the idea kept growing. I hope you enjoy this sketch of a beautiful village as much as I have had pleasure in producing it.

Richard H.Pearson
Welton 1996

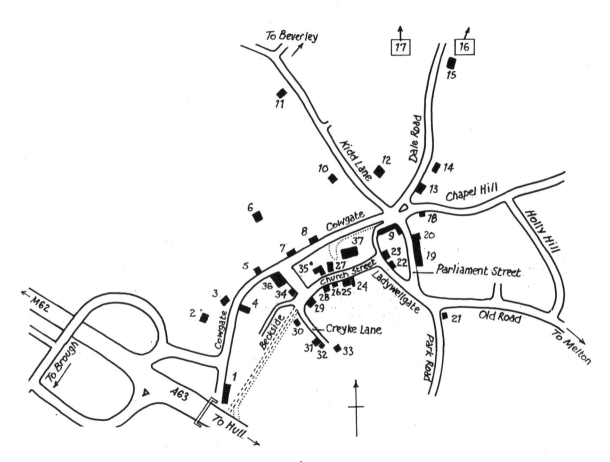

To Beverley

17

16

15

11

Kidd Lane

Dale Road

10

12

14

13   Chapel Hill

6

Cowgate

8

18

Holly Hill

7

9

37

20

23

19

5

35

27

22

Church Street

Parliament Street

36

34

Ladywellgate

26 25   24

M62

3

28

Cowgate

33

Beckside

4

29

21   Old Road

2

30

Creyke Lane

Park Road

To Brough

31   32

To Melton

1

A63

To Hull

4

LOCATIONS

I have placed the drawings in a sequence which can be followed on a walk round the village for those who might wish to look at the actual subjects. Starting with No.1 (Welton Garth) and so on, penultimately to No.36 (The Green Dragon Inn). Check your timing for opening hours! Duly refreshed you will be ready to appreciate the beauty of No.37 (St.Helen's Church).

WELTON AND THE BROADLEY FAMILY

In any reference to Welton's past, mention must be made of the influence of the Broadley family. It is a name which frequently appears in this book.

Thomas Broadley was a seventeenth century Hull merchant who founded the family which became the well known landowners of nineteenth century East Yorkshire. The first Broadley to be the major landowner in Welton was Henry.

Henry Broadley lived at Melton Hill between 1822 and 1836 when he bought Welton House. This became the family seat. Welton House was demolished in 1952. The Broadley estates were said to cover a large part of the East Riding during Henry's lifetime.

When Henry died in 1851 the property passed to his unmarried sister Sophia who herself died in 1864. Welton House and the estate then passed to Willam Henry Harrison(1820-1896) who changed the family name to Harrison-Broadley. William Henry Harrison-Broadley was a colonel in the Yorkshire Hussars, a J.P., High Sheriff and Conservative M.P. for the East Riding from 1868 to 1885.

William Henry left his estate to his nephew Henry Broadley Harrison-Broadley who was born in 1853. He married an American, Belle Tracy and from 1872 until 1892 lived in the U.S.A. He died in 1914.

On Henry's death the estate passed to his only son John Broadley Harrison-Broadley who lived at Tickton Grange, Beverley. When he died in 1946 at the age of 66 the estate began to be broken up.

WELTON GARTH is probably the best known landmark for the village for travellers on the A63 road. Its white frontage and variety of buildings are a familiar sight on the approach eastward towards Hull. It is in fact a collection of several adjoining cottages made into a single property. The enclosure Survey of 1772 tells of one cottage owned by William Hall, another by William Masham, another by Thomas Cook and a 'homestead' owned by Humphrey Appleton. By 1830 a Hull merchant, John Smith had acquired the various properties from which he made a single house.

As one enters the village at the western end WELTON GRANGE in Cowgate occupies a prominent site as warrants its importance as one of Welton's finest houses.

It was built during the 1740's of brown limestone. The owner at the time, Thomas Fell of Bingley, West Yorkshire may have built the house as we see it today but an earlier one is recorded. By 1770 it was owned by a Hull merchant, Richard Bell, and another merchant, John Carrick bought the house in 1794.

By 1834 Welton Grange was owned by Robert Raikes the Hull banker and after his death his widow, Anne owned the house. When she died in 1848 Henry Broadley bought the property which was let to a variety of professional people including John Wilkinson Esq., a prominent Hull solicitor.

In the twentieth century Welton Grange was used as a convalescent home for wounded officers during the 1914-1918 war and during the later 1940's it housed a toy factory!

The danger that Welton Grange might become a victim of decay in the late twentieth century was fortunately averted when it became the headquarters of the Stadium company, the house and grounds receiving careful restoration.

RICHARD H PEARSON ©

Further along Cowgate, just beyond the gateway to Welton Grange stands the substantial property which was once the house belonging to BARTRAM'S FARM. Not many years ago this was in a state of disrepair as the farm itself was long gone, the outbuildings which once fronted onto Cowgate having made way for modern houses.

The development to the rear of the farmhouse was named "Bartram's" as a reminder of the past. The company which owned the old farmyard saw fit to restore the farmhouse and it now makes an attractive feature on the approach to the village. There are two houses adjacent to each other; in its original form the farmhouse was to the right of the building whilst that to the left was a farm cottage.

The upper and lower left windows in the end wall are well executed dummies and one wonders how many window cleaners have been frustrated by these.

RICHARD H PEARSON

No.28 COWGATE, opposite to Bartram's is a beautiful house with a small but delightful garden. As it is set 'end-on' to the road it is largely unseen by the passer-by. The upper windows and roof give a hint of the house's quality and these are clearly visible.

The carefully maintained garden is one of many in a village of beautiful gardens and that of No.28 is high on the list of those to visit during the annual Garden Festival.

RICHARD H PEARSON ©

13

No.21 COWGATE was once the premises of one of Welton's blacksmiths, Mr John Bousfield. Although there are no clues that this house was used for such a business, the forge was in the room to the right of the front door with access through an entrance in the gable end where there is now a window. A side entry gave access to the yard and outbuildings at the rear. The house used to be part of the Broadley estate, later passing into the ownership of the blacksmith's descendants.

Blacksmiths were an essential presence in rural villages like Welton and in the 1840's William Nelson and John Parkinson fulfilled this duty. Early in the twentieth century Welton still had two blacksmiths, Mr Bousfield and Richard Nelson who was also the Parish Clerk. The premises of the other blacksmith were at the junction of Kidd Lane with Cowgate, long ago demolished.

RICHARD H PEARSON

15

The first impression one gains of WELTON MANOR as seen from Cowgate, is of a very attractive old house set in a beautiful garden. Meticulously maintained, it is a garden which looks good on even the bleakest winter day.

In the late eighteenth century the house was owned by Thomas Williamson, a wealthy Hull merchant. It was rebuilt by a later owner, Robert Raikes senior. In the early 1800's Raikes was the principal landowner in Welton and it was he who objected to a railway station being built for the village in 1840, so it was sited at Brough instead. The railway was only allowed to pass over Raikes' land when he was paid £10,000.

Welton Manor was formerly known as 'Spring Hill' and after being owned by Raikes and his widow Anne, the house was sold to Henry Broadley around 1848. Broadley was Conservative M.P. for the East Riding from 1837 until his death in 1851. He was also the first Chairman of the Hull & Selby Railway Company during the time of rail expansion.

One wonders if the gardens of Welton Manor were as well cared for in the days of Raikes and Broadley as they are today.

Richard H Pearson ©

Overlooking the Green is Barn House, an attractive brick house fronting on to Cowgate. This older property is all that remains of a row of similar contemporary buildings long since demolished to make way for what is now St.Helen's Flats. To the right of Barn House is the hairdresser's business, the premises of which were once a butcher's shop. The small door beside the entrance gave access to the butcher's yard to the rear.

To the right of this property where St.Helen's Flats now stand was once a complex of village businesses. Fronting on to Cowgate were shops, including the Post Office. To the rear was a yard wherein was a dance hall called The Pavilion, and the Imperial Cafe (prop. Mrs Sherer). There was also a fish and chips shop known to the locals as Walmsley's.

Barn House was once in the ownership of John Bartram, a butcher and farmer. Through the grounds of Barn House was piped the water for the fountain on the Green. The source of the water came from the springs in the grounds of Welton Manor. The owner of Welton Manor at the time was Charles England and he had a dispute with Bartram who severed the water pipe. The fountain has never flowed since.

RICHARD H. PEARSON ©

19

THE MEMORIAL HALL in Cowgate, along with the adjacent Welfare Club, could best be described as being the social centre of Welton, a familiar rendezvous for residents and visitors alike.

In earlier times the building was a dwelling owned by the Broadley estate and later used as the Estate Hall. Today it is dedicated to those who fought and fell in the two World Wars.

In September 1954 the Hull Daily Mail published the following:-
"50 YEARS AGO: September 1904. Colonel Harrison-Broadley of Welton Hall (sic) had for some time past intended to present Welton with a public hall and that intention is now to be carried out, plans having been prepared and a site chosen.

The donor recently bought Dr.Jackson's house at Welton for about £1,150 and it is proposed to utilise this in connection with the new hall which is to be made of corrugated iron. It is proposed to convert the house so as to make the front portion a suitable frontage for the hall."

After the 1939-45 war the building was bought by the village from the Broadley estate, funds being raised through concerts, dances and other events. The first steward was the late Mr Ralph Widd who was a prominent member of Welton Cricket Club and popular resident of the village.

RICHARD H PEARSON ©

21

'Just across the water' at the eastern end of Cowgate is the row of cottage properties forming BROOKSIDE. In recent years these have undergone alterations or modification but as this work was carried out with care and awareness of their visual importance such activity has proved successful.

The larger property to the right in the drawing is of an interesting design with a curiously angled gable end. It was once occupied by the village tailor, Mr Groom.

In the days when Welton had farms at the heart of the village such as Home Farm or Bartrams, livestock were driven to the pastures out of the village. On their return they would walk along the brook to wash and drink.

RICHARD H PEARSON

23

WELTON RISE in Kidd Lane is another of the houses in the village which is largely unseen by the passer-by. It is notable as having been the vicarage prior to the property of a more recent date.

The house is of red brick and dates from the early twentieth century but on this site and much earlier stood a more primitive 'vicarage house'. Thompson's "Welton" records the following in a Terrier of 1809:-

"The vicarage house is twenty-six yards in length and seven in breadth; it is built with white and grey stones and covered with thatch; it is two storeys high. A stable thirteen yards long and six wide built with white and grey stones and thatched. Two tithe barns both built with stones and thatched, one of them is twenty-five yards long and ten wide, the other fourteen yards long and seven wide."

RICHARD H PEARSON

25

WELTON HILL in Kidd Lane ranks as one of Welton's most attractive and important houses. It is of a shy disposition however, hiding itself behind a high wall by the roadside and set in wooded grounds. The passer-by may only glimpse the upper windows of this beautiful house.

Welton Hill was built around 1818 when Mary Galland acquired the site. Being on a hillside above the village it would have had fine views over the River Humber and surrounding countryside before the high trees obscured this. Mary Galland died in 1840 but her son, the Reverend Thomas Galland (died 1843) and his widow Frances (died 1867) lived at the house.

An intrinsic part of the setting of Welton Hill is the open aspect to the south from which the drawing is taken. The house overlooks a meadow beyond the garden which contributes to the overall seclusion of the house. One hopes that this tranquil setting remains as it is and modern development never spoils this viewpoint.

Not long ago it seemed that WELTON HALL was doomed and it might have been demolished to make way for modern development. For years this important property had lain hidden amid its jungle of untended grounds at the western end of Dale Road. Although divided into flats at that time its future appeared to be bleak.

Thankfully the building was saved when it was acquired in the 1980's by the Hull company, Fenner PLC as their headquarters. The result has been a remarkable and admirable restoration.

In 1764 Welton Hall was owned by a Hull grocer, William Battle. He died in 1790 and the house became the property of George Whitaker a 'Welton gentlemen'. By 1796 it was owned by a Scottish surgeon, James Wood of Perth. It passed on to the ownership of a Hull merchant, Peter Bulmer by 1800 and then to a brewer, John Richardson in 1803. By 1818 James Lowthrop, a Welton cornfactor was the owner. Later Welton Hall was the property of Sir William Lowthrop until his death in 1853.

Sir William Lowthrop was Mayor of Hull in 1839-1840 when he presented Queen Victoria with an address of congratulation on her escape from assassination. In the early twentieth century Welton Hall was the residence of Samuel Pilling Esq., J.P.

In the late twentieth century not many properties of the size of Welton Hall can survive due to the cost of their upkeep so Welton is fortunate in having its most important buildings preserved for future generations.

RICHARD H PEARSON

Set at the eastern end of the village WELTON LODGE overlooks 'Top Green'. It is without doubt one of Welton's most beautiful houses and it is to the village's advantage that careful and extensive restoration has rescued it from increasing decay.

In the Enclosures Survey of 1772 the site was owned by Dr William Welfit who was vicar of Welton at the time. Welfit moved on to Canterbury in 1787 having appointed his curate, the Reverend Miles Popple. Popple himself apparently moved into the house wherein he lived until his death in 1846 at the age of 90. He obviously thrived on the healthy Welton air.

Popple's youngest daughter Anne lived on at the house until she died in 1872 at the age of 73. Anne's memorial is to be seen on the village Green, the stone fountain which bears her name.

RICHARD H PEARSON ©

31

THE OLD STABLES in Dale Road is a property not fully visible from the gateway. At this entrance is found the Cattle Well, one of the numerous sources from which Weltonians took fresh water before the advent of a piped supply.

The property is a conversion into a house from the stable block belonging to Welton Lodge. Previously it consisted of a coach house, tack room and stabling. Its conversion was completed after the Second World War when in the ownership of the late Wing Commander J.H.Thompson D.F.C., A.F.C., D.L.

The Cattle Well within the stable yard is supplied from the springs and was first harnessed by the owner of Welton Lodge, John Ferrands Esq., in 1743. By 1832 the well was in need of repair and this was done by the then owner, the Reverend Miles Popple who probably erected the stack pipes around the village which were fed from the Cattle Well. Few houses in Welton had piped water even after the 1939-45 war and residents had to use this water or the stack pipes with the inevitable labour of carrying water in all weather at all seasons.

RICHARD H PEARSON

33

There were once three watermills in Welton but only WELTON WATERMILL in Dale Road remains, although in a sad state of decay. One of these mills was reputedly destroyed by fire in the days of Charles I. The second mill stood in the centre of the village until its last remaining buildings were demolished in 1967. The remaining watermill that we can see today was built in 1862.

Around 1894 the milling family of Thompson took over the leasehold of the watermill in Dale Road from the Broadley estate. Mr Frank Ling was the Manager and the mill ground grain for local farmers. When Frank Ling died in 1944 his son Ted became the Manager. The watermill was bought from the Broadley estate and a limited company was formed.

In the 1960's small millers were taken over by the large concerns and when Welton mill ceased operations in 1966 the land and buildings were sold. Thus for thirty years this important part of Welton's history has stood derelict, the nearby mill-dam choked with debris. Local people have many memories of the mill in its heyday including the strong man who could carry a sack of grain under each arm as he climbed the ladder to the hopper.

On the hillside behind the watermill once stood a windmill, traces of which remain in the uneven turf. This mill was in operation until about 1849 and an idea of what it looked like can be had from a watercolour of Welton in the Leeds City Art Gallery by the great artist John Sell Cotman. The picture dates from 1803.

RICHARD H PEARSON

One of the many pleasant walks to be enjoyed in Welton is that which travels along Dale Road and on into Welton Dale, the road gradually leaving suburbia and entering the beauty and tranquillity of the Dale.

It is a surprising fact that before 1772 when it became a private occupation road, Dale Road was the main route from Welton to Beverley. This ran through Welton Dale and Wauldby Dale to Little Weighton. After 1772 the road which replaced it was that which runs North of the village to Riplingham cross-roads.

As one enters the wooded part of Dale Road beside the lake one passes DALE COTTAGE. This is in an idyllic situation at the very gateway to the Dale itself. The cottage once housed the gamekeeper for the Broadley estate, and as contemporary photographs verify, it was once possible to obtain a cup of tea here when taking a walk.

RICHARD H PEARSON

37

Set in the woods at the north-east end of Welton Dale lies the RAIKES MAUSOLEUM. Although on private land and not accessible to the public, glimpses of this interesting building can be had from the path nearby during the time of year when foliage does not obstruct the view.

The mausoleum was built in 1819 by Robert Raikes senior, for the members of his family. Raikes was an important man in Welton's history as he was a major landowner in the early nineteenth century.

Born in 1765 Raikes became a prominent banker in Hull and married Anne, the only daughter of Thomas Williamson a Welton landowner and owner of Welton House. When Williamson died in 1809 Raikes inherited Welton House and other property. On Raike's death in 1837 his widow lived on at Welton House which had been much altered by her husband. Robert Raikes junior lived at East Dale House, the site of which is now South Hunsley School. Both this house and Welton House were long ago demolished.

Later on much of the land and property owned by the Raikes family came into the ownership of the Broadley estate.

RICHARD H. PEARSON ©

39

RICHARD H PEARSON

40

No.1 CHAPEL HILL overlooks 'Top Green' and is the one remaining property of a row of dwellings that has survived the post-war demolition which made way for the new houses on Chapel Hill.

The original part of this cottage is to the right of the fall-pipe in the drawing. To the left a modern, carefully matching extension has been added.

A interesting and attractive detail can be seen over the door. This is a carving of a head, the subject of which is unclear and the origin unknown.

RICHARD H PEARSON

42

PARLIAMENT STREET today cannot be viewed without care as it is part of the one-way traffic system and the pedestrian must be on guard for the frequent passage of vehicles. With this in mind a walk along Parliament Street is rewarding for it contains a terrace of cottages of uniform and interesting design. Originally occupied by the employees of the Broadley estate they are now private residences and retain their essential character in spite of cosmetic alterations.

With care for passing traffic one should note the amazing chimney stacks of this terrace. Built in a time when craftsmanship was of a greater value than time and money these chimneys are a treasured legacy. Viewed across the village from Kidd Lane they make a remarkable feature.

The modern development known as Raikes Court to the rear of Parliament Street was the site of the Broadley estate yard once dominated by a large chimney of a similar pattern to the chimneys mentioned above. Latterly there was a caravan factory on this site.

No.9 PARLIAMENT STREET at its North end was once the Police Station. It is an interesting building visually as well as historically. In conjunction with this building was the Justice Room which existed at the junction of Ladywellgate with Church Street, known as Turner's Yard. Here sat the Magistrate's Court "on the first Saturday in the month, at 10a.m."

Although the village no longer has a resident policeman, in earlier times the place seems to have been overrun with gentlemen in dark blue. In 1905 John Walker was police superintendent along with 3 sergeants and 14 constables. This was not due to the excessive lawlessness of Weltonians but because Welton was at the heart of a large rural police area.

To the rear of No.9, across the yard, was the cell block where prisoners were kept prior to an appearance before the Magistrates. The Minutes of the Quarter Sessions of June 1866 read:-"From the Chief Constable, Lt.Col.B.Granville:'to name to the Police Committee the unhealthy state of the prisoners' cells at Welton, together with the defiency of water and the fact that the clothes and rugs used by the superintendent and prisoners who have died from fever have all been destroyed.'"

In later times a new, smaller police house was built in Dale Road on land once part of the Broadley estate. Now the village has no resident policeman - a victim of modern economics.

WESTERN LODGE at the junction of Park Road with Old Road is all that remains as evidence of the existence of Welton House, one of the 'grand' houses of the village which was demolished in 1952. At the eastern side of Welton House there once existed two other lodges.

Around 1770 the then owner of Welton House, Thomas Williamson, decided that the road to Hull passed too close to Welton House so he had it realigned. The sharp, inclined bend of Old Road just outside Western Lodge is a reminder of Williamson's influence.

RICHARD H PEARSON ©

46

No.3 LADYWELLGATE is a fine property at the corner of Ladywellgate with Church Street. It was once the residence, early in the twentieth century of Dr. Millar. He is described as; "surgeon, medical officer and public vaccinator for Welton district of Sculcoates union and medical referee for Scottish Amicable & Mutual of New York Insurance Companies". Dr. Millar had his own chauffeur who lived further along Ladywellgate.

The house, on its street side is of a simple and straightforward design which is most attractive. Unseen by the public, the rear is a fascinating ramble of interesting details and amendments, all of which add to the character of the house. There is also a charming 'English' garden with foxgloves and roses.

© RICHARD H PEARSON

The delightful white-rendered house known as THE COTTAGE stands at the eastern end of Church Street. Although named 'The Cottage' this is in fact a sizeable property with an attractive, secluded garden. The house was once the residence of a well known local solicitor, Frank Jackson Esq.

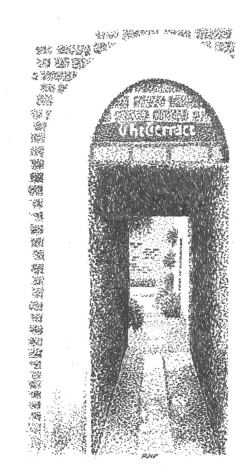

THE TERRACE in Church Street is a narrow passage leading to cottages. Here resided members of the staff of the Broadley estate among whom were two cowmen. two grooms, a joiner, a gamekeeper and a chauffeur. The Estate had a staff in excess of 100.

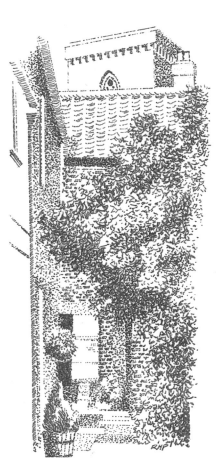

THE POST OFFICE in Church Street along with the hairdressing business in Cowgate are the remnants of the numerous shops and services in the village. Over the years the Post Office has had several locations and the present building is very distinctive. It may not be an architectural classic but it possesses some interesting.detail, being at the gable end of a building which forms one side of The Terrace.

In the 1840's Welton's Post Office was at the grocery and drapery business of Anthony Wallis, the exact location is not known. In those days letters dispatched to Hull at 8.30 in the morning arrived in Hull by 6 p.m. the same day.

Ninety years ago Mr Appleton was the Welton sub-postmaster. As well as also running a refreshment 'pavilion' off Cowgate he was kept busy with a postal service bringing letters via Brough every day at 6.35 in the morning each weekday and at 4.05 in the afternoons. Post left the village at 11 a.m. and 6.50 p.m.

Mr Appleton was also responsible for a Sunday post at 2.50 p.m. No doubt he took an early Sunday lunch.

RICHARD H PEARSON ©

51

It is difficult today to imagine Welton having numerous shops, however until the mid-twentieth century this was the case. The largest shop was that of Francis Myers in Church Street, next to Creyke House. This business was a general store selling food, clothing and hardware. Many Weltonians remember Myers' with affection and rue the day its imposing premises were demolished. Myers supplied nearby villages and farms with goods, having an efficient delivery service.

There were numerous smaller shops including sweetshops, butchers and cobblers. 150 years ago Welton could boast 4 shoemakers, 3 butchers, 2 plumbers and glaziers, 4 drapers and tailors as well as a linen maker, 4 joiners and wheelwrights as well as grocers.

In the 1930's Welton was still rich in shops and other trades. Mrs Stathers had the Post Office and Stationers, Richard Johnson was the saddler, Mr Darby the joiner and undertaker and Leonard Train had the shop which later became Williamson's as seen in the drawing.

This drawing of WILLIAMSON'S SHOP in Church Street will revive memories of the friendly and convenient store. It ceased trading some years ago and is now converted into cottages.

SMOOTINGS is the property which lies between Church Street and The Green. The name is believed to derive from a local word 'Smoot' or 'Smout', a 'smoot' being a hole in a hedge in the track of a hare, a 'smout' being a bolt hole. This may apply to Smootings with regard to its situation twixt Church Street and The Green.

Here was once the site of one of Welton's watermills. This was 'the mill in the Town', the other being the 'mill in the Dale'. This watermill ceased its activity in the latter half of the nineteenth century, its last remaining buildings demolished in the 1960's. Perhaps this was the workplace of Thomas Stephenson, described as a corn miller in the directory of 1845.

SHAWS HOUSE in Church Street was once a school run by two ladies, the Misses Shaw. Their father was a veterinary surgeon who specialised in the treatment of horses. Shaws House served as both school and surgery, no doubt with interesting results.

CREYKE HOUSE stands at the junction of Church Street with Creyke Lane. It is a fine property to look at and has played an important role in Welton's history. .Around 1772 there were two cottages on this site but by 1778 Thomas Hudson, a Hull painter and glazier, built a house here. By 1791 it was owned by a Hull merchant, John Newmarch, who then sold it to William Bell Esq. in 1793. By 1812 Creyke House was the property of the Reverend Kingsman Basket who was Master of Hull Charterhouse. When he died in 1833 he was succeeded by Roger Basket as the owner and on his death in 1841 Creyke House was eventually acquired by Sophia Broadley in 1855.

As part of the Broadley estate and funded by H.B.Harrison-Broadley, the house became a school. In 1905 this establishment was attended by 50 boys, 40 girls and 30 infants. The Headmaster was Mr Enoch Boardman who was aided by Miss Gertrude Dorsey who took charge of the infants. Mr Boardman was also the Registrar of births and deaths at that time. Later Mr Boardman's son, Edward also taught at Creyke House and was Parish Clerk.

A new County Primary School was built in Common Lane around 1912 and Creyke House ceased to be a school, reverting to a private house.

The building which stands at the head of Creyke Lane could never be described as beautiful or an architectural gem. It is best described as 'functional' and was built to serve the village in several capacities.

Known to Weltonians as the FORESTERS' HALL or sometimes the Oddfellows' Hall it was once the meeting place for the Order of Foresters which was an early type of Friendly Society. Active early in the twentieth century, numerous prominent Welton residents were members and they came from a variety of trades and professions.

When there was a school at Creyke House nearby, the Hall was used as the infant annex and evidence of this can still be seen in the remains of derelict buildings at the rear of the Hall and the overgrown playground.

Mid century the Hall was anonymously purchased and donated to the village as a Church Hall and so became the location for numerous social activities until these transferred to the Memorial Hall in Cowgate and the Foresters' Hall was left unused.

RICHARD H PEARSON

59

CREYKE LODGE is arguably the most imposing house in Creyke Lane. At one time this property was in fact two houses and behind its high wall lies another of Welton's attractive gardens.

Creyke Lane is tucked away to the south-east of Welton Green and it is interesting to note that it was once a through-road leading out of the village in the late eighteenth century. Thomas Thompson's book of 1869 tells us:-

"There was an old lane called 'Crake Lane'...which lane ran through the south lawn of Welton House and no one soon after came to have any interest in it but Thomas Williamson, through purchases made by him, so it has been thrown into and now forms part of the lawn of Welton House".

This was at the time of the Enclosures of the 1770's and thus Creyke (or Crake) Lane ceased to be a thoroughfare out of the village and eventually became the cul-de-sac we know today.

JASMINE COTTAGE in Creyke Lane is a conversion of another of Welton's long-gone shops. In this instance the premises of Mr Vincent Giddy, a pork butcher. Its position was obviously well away from the main 'shopping centre' of the village but no doubt if Mr Giddy's chops were good they were worth the walk round the corner.

At the end of Creyke Lane and set within its own grounds lies PARK HOUSE. This was once the house occupied by the Head Gardener for the Broadley estate and the garden is a remnant of the very extensive grounds of Welton House which were maintained by a small army of under gardeners.

No. 4 THE GREEN occupies a prominent position close by The Green Dragon Inn. It is of a simple yet most attractive design.

Situated to the south-east corner of The Green the property was once the farmhouse of Home Farm. The old farmyard and outbuildings lay to the rear in what is today the modern development known as Beckside. The farm had the local name of 'Parkinson's yard', the origin of which seems uncertain but could be connected with the village blacksmith of the early 1800's, John Parkinson.

In the 1930's this farm was very busy and threshing was undertaken by means of a steam traction engine. Here was also a fine herd of cattle which grazed on the slopes above Chapel Hill. These animals were under the control of the cowkeeper, Dick Gibbs.

The house was once one of the many places accommodating the Post Office and until the 1960's the premises to the rear were a riding school prior to the Beckside development.

RICHARD H PEARSON ©

The familiar view across THE GREEN shows the houses where, on the left was once Penrose's shop which sold freshly baked bread and confectionery. The house to the right replaced earlier thatched cottages which became the village Poor House in the nineteenth century. At one time the Green was much smaller and without the many trees we have today.

The fountain on the Green was donated by Anne Popple, daughter of the Reverend Popple who came to Welton in 1787.

Water was supplied from Spring Hill which is now Welton Manor. The inscription, though abbreviated reads:-

"In memory of Anne Popple A.D. 1874. I will give a vow God, that if you have a thirst of the fountain of the water of life, drink freely."

The fountain is an attractive feature with many fine details, though much eroded. It would be wonderful to see Anne's gift to the village flow again.

THE GREEN DRAGON is well known to many who are not Welton residents. Its historic association with Dick Turpin is well recorded but it is doubtful if the highwayman would recognise the place today should his ghost return. There have been many alterations to the Inn in recent years.

The Dragon was once one of three Inns in Welton. The Fleece was in Cowgate, behind the Green Dragon and The Board Inn was in Parliament Street.

In the 1840's the landlord of the Dragon was John Wright.. An Eleanor Wright, possibly his wife, is described as a 'chaise owner' and probably took care of local transport arrangements for customers. The Dragon was a staging post on the old Hull Road and the Rodney Coach passed through at 7.30 each morning and returned at 4 in the afternoon. William Hardbattle was on hand as a farrier and he also ran a beerhouse of his own. Henry Raynor was landlord at the Dragon in 1905 whilst the other village publicans were Mrs Haime and Mrs Harsley. The Green dragon was part of the Broadley estate until it was bought by the Hull Brewery after the 1939-45 war. In more recent times many will remember Mr Norman Marsh who was the landlord until the Inn became part of the Mansfield Brewery organisation.

The position which ST. HELEN'S CHURCH occupies at the heart of Welton is particularly attractive. In many ways a typical 'English' setting overlooking the village Green, Mill-dam and weeping willows.

The history of the church may be read elsewhere but its restoration in the nineteenth century was visually significant.

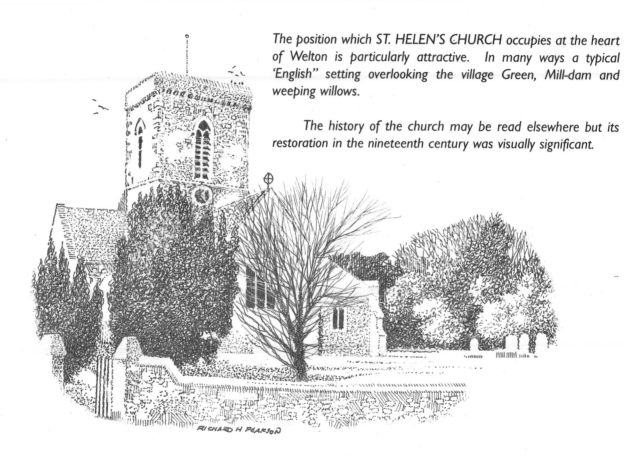

RICHARD H PEARSON

Prior to Sir George Gilbert Scott's restoration of the church in 1863 it had "a large embattled tower, terminated at the angles by crocketed pinnacles and vanes."

There are illustrations of how it looked, notably in J.S.Cotman's watercolour of 1803.There we see Welton's church with a much more complicated tower.

The restoration of 1863 was funded by Sophia Broadley but that of recent times was a united public effort which was organised by a devoted and hard working team. Thus everyone who appreciates the beauty and significance of this building can enjoy it for years to come.

St Helen's Church details: The Vestry doorway on the north side and (right) the remarkable chimney pots.